What Does it Mean to be 'Green'?

Sustainability, Respect & Spirituality

Neil Paul Cummins

Vitae Publications

A catalogue record for this book is available from the British Library

ISBN: 978-1-907962-13-4

Published by Vitae Publications

Reading, England

For Thomas

Contents

Preface

For many years I have been thinking about the nature of two relationships. Firstly, the relationship that exists between the human species and the rest of the life-forms that reside on the Earth. Secondly, the relationship that exists between life on Earth and the rest of the universe.

When one considers these relationships one can reach conclusions which at first glance appear to be counterintuitive. What I mean by this is that if one doesn't consider the nature of these two relationships then one might find the answers to certain questions to be obvious; however, when one starts pondering these relationships then one can come to realise that the answers to these questions are far from obvious. Indeed, one might become convinced that what one previously thought were 'obvious' answers are actually wrong.

I assume that one question which has a seemingly obvious answer is: What does it mean to be 'green'? In this book I consider this question from the perspective of the two relationships outlined above. This perspective leads me to conclude that the seemingly obvious answer is far too simplistic. Indeed, on reading this book you might conclude that the seemingly obvious answer is wrong. You might also conclude that there are two different answers to the question; if so, then whether the seemingly obvious answer is wrong will depend on exactly what the question means. At the very least I hope that this book stimulates you to start reflecting for yourself on the various possible answers to the question of what it means to be 'green'.

'

Introduction

My consideration of the question of what it means to be 'green' is centred on the phenomena of sustainability, respect and spirituality. In the first part of the book – *What Does it Mean to be 'Green'?* – I focus on sustainability and respect. I outline a broad and a narrow conception of sustainability and I consider how these two conceptions relate to respect for other life-forms.

The narrow conception of sustainability is focused solely on the human realm, whereas the broad conception is focused on the totality of life on Earth. Is acting in a sustainable way sufficient for being 'green? According to the broad conception of sustainability it is, but when we come to the narrow conception of sustainability things are more complex. One might think that – on the 'narrow conception' – if the impacts of the human species were 'neutral'/sustainable then the human species would be acting in a 'green' way. However, I suggest that a human can only be considered to be 'green' if they have a particular attitude – an attitude of respect towards other life-forms. So, if all humans lacked this attitude then the human species wouldn't be acting in a 'green' way, even if its impacts were 'neutral'/sustainable.

In the second part of the book – *'Green' Spirituality* – I consider in greater detail the

12

relationship that exists between an individual human and the rest of the life-forms that reside on the Earth. There is a way of living, a way of being in the world, a way of seeing the universe, which can be considered to be 'green'. This attitude to the non-human realm is the attitude of 'green spirituality'. It is an attitude which is grounded in an appreciation of the evolving nature of the universe and the place of the human species in such a universe.

I consider how the attitude of 'green spiritual-ity' accords with the broad notion of sustainability that is outlined in the first part of the book. In so doing I am drawn to coin a new term to describe the great value that the human species – via its technology – has for the future sustainability of life on Earth. This term is 'green-tech spirituality'. In the final pages of the book I outline what I believe to be the central tenets of the 'green-tech spirituality' paradigm.

What Does it Mean to be 'Green'?

In the early twenty-first century the 'green movement' is growing in strength. Of this I am sure.
But what exactly does it mean to be 'green'? One
probably assumes that one is being 'green' when one
decides to ride one's bicycle rather than drive one's
car. One probably assumes that one is being 'green'
when one takes a shower rather than a bath. And,
one probably assumes that one is being 'green' when
one takes one's own bags to the supermarket to
bring one's shopping home in.

These examples seem to indicate that being 'green' is typically associated with using fewer resources. The fewer resources one uses the more 'green' one is. This conclusion is reinforced by the widely discussed 'carbon footprint' which outlines how much carbon one's lifestyle uses. This conception of being 'green' underpins the 'green movement'. The 'green movement' is a movement whose central underlying assumption is that being 'green' means reducing the impacts that the human species has on the Earth. So, on this view, being 'green' means having a *lower* carbon footprint, consuming *less* resources, buying *less*, driving *less* and flying *less*; all human impacts need to be reduced.

These initial thoughts concerning *what it is to be 'green'* are surely very simplistic. One would probably not want to say that a person was living a 'green' life simply because they used very few resources. A person could use very few resources but spend their days torturing animals. Such a person is surely not living a 'green' lifestyle. This implies that a 'green' lifestyle involves having a certain level of respect for living entities – a certain attitude *which leads to* certain actions.

So, perhaps the core of being 'green' is a particular attitude towards life? The term 'green' surely arose because we are surrounded by living plants and trees which are coloured green. So, perhaps being 'green' is *acting in a way which is in the interests of all of the life-forms which exist on the Earth*. Contrarily, being 'not green' is acting in a human-centered way, with the interests of non-human life-forms discarded. More generally, being 'not green' is simply acting in a way *which is **not** in the interests of all of the life-forms which exist on the Earth*.

If this is right then it opens a whole 'can of worms'. For, can humans really know for certain what is in the interests of all of the life-forms which exist on the Earth? At a more general level, can humans know for certain what is in the interests of that part of the universe that is life on Earth?

One would assume that all life-forms would like to be treated with respect. One would also assume that these life-forms would like to survive rather than perish. If this is right, then being 'green' would mean acting in a way which is respectful to all life-forms *and* which helps to aid the survival of all life-forms.

So, one can see why the widespread belief that being 'green' entails reducing human impacts/ resource use has arisen. One might assume that reducing human resource use leads to sustainability, and that sustainability aids the survival of all life-forms. But, is this right? And if this is right in itself, does it miss the wood for the trees?

It is surely true that for all life-forms to survive there needs to be sustainability. But what exactly is sustainability? Talk of sustainability often gets translated into talk of minimising the human impact on the Earth. So, on this view, if every human action on the Earth was (let us imagine) offset by an opposing action then there would be sustainability. By this I mean, if the effect of the human species on the Earth was 'neutral' then there would be sustainability. This is a 'narrow' conception of sustainability because it is focused solely on the impacts/actions of the human species. It is assumed that if human impacts are sufficiently low, or if human actions are 'neutral' on the Earth, that there will be sustainability.

There is a much wider application of the notion of sustainability. From this 'broader' perspective sustainability isn't about minimising (even eradicating/neutralising) human impacts, it is about the biosphere of the Earth continuing to exist in a state which can sustain complex life-forms. When we see that this is really what sustainability (and being 'green') is about then we can ask the question of which human actions might contribute to this sustainability. When we do this we find that there are diverse, and possibly unexpected, ways of living which might possibly be 'green' ways of living. When I use the term 'sustainability' from now on I will be using it in this broader 'entire biosphere of the

Earth' sense, rather than to refer simply to 'human impacts/resource use'.

It is possible to believe that if the human species used minimal resources that this would result in sustainability (recall that the term 'sustainability' is now being used to refer to the *sustainability of life on Earth* and not to refer to the minimisation/eradication of human impacts). Indeed, this is the standard view. However, if one takes a broader evolutionary perspective then it is far from clear that such a reduction would contribute to sustainability. You might find this to be very counter-intuitive, so let me outline the evolutionary background which leads to this conclusion.

From an evolutionary perspective we can get a different perspective on what sustainability is. Let me remind you that sustainability *is about the biosphere of the Earth continuing to exist in a state which can sustain complex life-forms.* So, we need to understand how the biosphere of the Earth operates if we are to understand how sustainability can be achieved.

From an evolutionary perspective we can see that in the past the biosphere of the Earth was not able to sustain complex life-forms; there was a point in the evolution of the Earth when the biosphere of the Earth first became able to sustain complex life-forms. How did the biosphere evolve the ability to sustain complex life-forms? The answer is that non-complex life-forms changed the biosphere of the Earth in order to make it habitable for complex life-forms.

This transition from non-complex life-forms to complex life-forms can be seen as a transition that contributes to sustainability (as we will see a little later, the emergence of complex life-forms is required for the long-term sustainability of non-complex life-forms). Sustainability shouldn't be seen as just applying to the human realm; as we have seen it applies to the entire biosphere of the Earth. Since complex-life forms evolved they have themselves been acting in a way that contributes to sustainability. Along with non-complex life-forms, complex life-forms have been regulating the conditions of the biosphere to keep them favourable for their continued existence. In other words, both before the evolution of the human species, and since that evolution, the life-forms of the Earth have been acting in a way that ensures sustainability. So, this means that these life-forms have been acting in a 'green' way.

I should, perhaps, say a few words concerning the phrase *acting in a 'green' way*. At the most fundamental level *all of the actions which result in the biosphere of the Earth continuing to exist in a state which can sustain complex life-forms are 'green' actions.* So, life on Earth has been acting in a 'green' way for millions of years. We have seen that there is a 'narrow' conception of sustainability which is concerned with minimising (ideally 'eliminating') human impacts on the Earth. This 'narrow conception' will have its own associated conception of 'green actions'; all actions which lead to a reduction in 'impact' will be 'green' actions. I have also suggested that acting in a 'green' way requires a certain 'respectful' attitude to other planetary life-forms; however, this attitude only applies to the 'narrow' conception of sustainability/'greenness'. For, if the achievement of sustainability at the 'broad level' required a 'disrespectful' attitude then such an attitude would be a 'green'/sustainable attitude at the fundamental/'broad' level. So, in effect, the 'respectful attitude' applies only to individual humans; whilst a range of attitudes are compatible with the achievement of sustainability. What this means (it is perhaps a little confusing) is that a range of attitudes can be 'green' attitudes, but that there is a single attitude which is a 'respectful green attitude'. The former range of attitudes are 'green' because of their contribution to the 'broad' conception of sustainability; the latter attitude is 'green' because it enshrines an individual humans respect and care for life on Earth.

Having made this detour into what are 'green' actions let us return to our consideration of those 'green' actions which have been occurring on the

Earth for millions of years: *life on Earth* acting in a way that ensures sustainability. Given this long evolutionary history of life on Earth acting in a sustainable fashion one has to wonder how the human species fits into this picture. Life has been acting sustainably for hundreds of millions of years and the human species is a very recent arrival to life on Earth. Could it be that life on Earth could now be acting in a non-sustainable way after hundreds of millions of years of acting in a sustainable way? That is to say, is that part of life on Earth which is the human species acting in an unsustainable way? Or, contrarily, could it be the case that the same pattern which has been ongoing for hundreds of millions of years is still ongoing? In other words, could it be that the human species is actually acting in a sustainable way?

To see why the human species could be acting in a sustainable way one truly needs to be engrained within the evolutionary perspective. One needs to imagine the creation of the solar system, the early days of our Sun, the creation of the Earth and the other planets of the solar system, and the origin of life on Earth.

The entire solar system needs to be seen as a forever changing and evolving whole. Let us first consider the evolving part of the whole that is the Sun. The Sun is the potentiality which enables life to arise in the solar system. When it was first formed the energy that it gave out was comparatively low. This means that there would have been no chance of life evolving on the Earth and the outer planets of the solar system. Life needs at least a certain amount of solar energy in order to evolve on a planet and these planets, being so far away from a weak Sun simply didn't have enough incoming solar energy.

However, over time the Sun gets hotter and the energy that it radiates out to the solar system thereby increases. This means that a time comes when the incoming solar radiation to planets such as the Earth and Mars is high enough to enable life to evolve. One could think of the universe as seeking to give rise to life wherever the conditions allow. In the past the time clearly came when the conditions on

Earth – due to the increasing output of the Sun – enabled life to evolve.

It is clear that life needs certain conditions in order to exist. Before the increase in the output of the Sun it was simply too cold on the Earth for life to exist. It is also the case that life (particularly complex life) cannot exist if the temperature is too hot. From the evolutionary perspective one might well be thinking that if the solar output continues to increase then the incoming solar radiation to the Earth will be too intense for life to survive. This straightforwardly follows from life needing a certain temperature range in order to survive and the output of the Sun continuing to increase. And, of course, the Sun will continue to get hotter and hotter until it finally explodes and expires.

So, the Sun is an evolving entity. Firstly, it enables life to evolve on the Earth. Secondly, it eradicates any life that exists on the Earth. The eradication of life is clearly incompatible with sustainability!

We have seen that when life first evolved the simple life-forms that existed changed the composition of the biosphere so that complex life-forms could evolve. One of the key elements of this enabling is that life has been regulating the temperature of the atmosphere in order to keep it within the narrow band within which complex life can survive. The output of the Sun has already increased by 25 per cent since life arose on the Earth (40 per cent overall) but the atmospheric temperature of the Earth has remained within the narrow band due to the regulation of the temperature by planetary life.

From this perspective we can see that the sustainability of life on Earth is primarily about this regulation. Without such regulation the temperature of the atmosphere would be too high for complex life-forms to survive. This means that actions which contribute to this regulation are sustainable actions ('green' actions), whilst actions which do not contribute to this regulation are not sustainable actions (they are 'non-green' actions).

Let us now consider how human actions fit into this scenario. Does the human use of planetary resources contribute to this regulation or not? That is to say, are human actions sustainable actions?

According to one view human actions do not contribute to this regulation because they risk disrupting the non-human regulatory mechanisms which have been ongoing for millions of years. So, by moving colossal amounts of fossil fuels from their burial place in the crust to the Earth's surface, atmosphere and oceans, one could think that humans are disrupting the non-human ability of life on Earth to regulate the temperature of the atmosphere. Indeed, by definition, some might think that this is unsustainable because such fuels are called non-renewable – and non-renewable implies 'unsustainable'. However, as we have noted this is part of the 'narrow' notion of sustainability, not the 'broad' one that is being used here.

According to another view human actions do contribute to this regulation. Indeed, according to this view human actions are an essential part of this regulation. So, high levels of human resource use would be an essential part of sustainability. How can this be? We have seen that the entire solar system is in a continuous state of evolution. The Sun's output increases over time, whilst simultaneously, life on Earth's strategy for maintaining the conditions it needs in order to exist (in the face of such an increase) changes over time. There is a delicate interplay between these two evolving entities. One needs to imagine that life on Earth is in some kind of struggle (even a battle or a war) against the Sun. Life is trying it's best to maintain the temperature of the Earth's atmosphere – to keep it down – whilst the Sun keeps sending out increasing amounts of solar energy to the Earth. Each increase in solar radiation is another offensive which needs to be defeated. Life on Earth is not all powerful, whilst the Sun is relentless; clearly, the time will come when the ability of life on Earth to fend off the assaults of the Sun will end. Many people (such as Sir James Lovelock) believe that the Earth is already in a very weak state – its regulatory ability having already significantly weakened. One can easily imagine that it is just a matter of time before the Sun is victorious and life on Earth has been more or less decimated. When the ability of life on Earth to regulate the temperature of the atmosphere fails planetary temperatures will shoot upwards and the over-whelming majority of life-forms will die.

Life on Earth has been marshalling its troops (its resources) as best it can to prolong the war for as long as possible. In this context we can get a different perspective on human resource use. Human resource use can be seen as simply the latest battle in this war. The human species can be seen as that part of life which has the ability to marshal the resources of the planet in astonishing ways. By bringing forth a resource user of such magnificence it is even possible that life on Earth might be victorious in its war against the Sun.

How can the human species defeat the mighty Sun on behalf of life on Earth? The answer is obvious. By marshalling the resources of the Earth the human species is able to continue the regulatory process of the Earth's atmosphere into the distant future. In the absence of human technology life on Earth has marshalled its own resources to regulate the temperature of the atmosphere for millions of years. That ability is now weakening. The continuation of this regulation requires a marshalling of such ingenuity that only a 'technological' part of life can achieve the feat. So, the human species can defeat the mighty Sun by using its technological ingenuity to regulate the temperature of the Earth's atmosphere. In so doing the human species would be ensuring the continued existence of life on Earth. In so doing the human species would be bringing sustainability to life on Earth. Therefore, the actions which bring about such a state of affairs are 'green' actions.

What, specifically, are these 'green' actions? All of the actions that enable the human species to become technological are 'green' actions. And, clearly, becoming technological is not something that happens overnight. In order to become technological a species needs to have a long period of tool use, a long period of exploration of its surroundings, and a prolonged period of intense resource use.

If the human species hadn't had a high level of resource use then it is hard to imagine how it could have become technological. Using resources, moulding and modifying resources, these are the bedrocks underlying the road to technology.

More fundamentally, the actions of the human species reflect the underlying nature of life on Earth and the underlying nature of the universe. As we have seen the whole evolution of life on Earth can be seen as one prolonged journey of *marshalling as many resources as possible* in order to maintain the conditions of the planet so that they are favourable for life. This 'marshalling of resources' is the nature of life. The human species is simply a part of life – it has this same nature. There is not anything 'wrong' or 'unnatural' about the human species using the resources of the Earth to ensure the future survival of life on Earth. Such resource use is surely the epitome of sustainability; the epitome of being 'green'.

What this means is that when one goes shopping and buys a lot of junk that one really doesn't need one is simply an expression of the desire of life to marshal as many resources as possible in order to survive. Such shopping isn't being 'not green' on this view of the universe and the place of humans in it.

Does this mean that to be 'green' is to use as many resources as possible? This would be much too simplistic a way of describing the situation. Being 'green' is best thought of as something which applies at the level of the human species (or even all of life on Earth). If the human species successfully regulates the temperature of the Earth's atmosphere then the human species is acting in the way that is in the best interests of life on Earth; it is ensuring the continued survival of life on Earth. The human actions that lead to this regulation should therefore be thought of as 'green' actions.

This doesn't mean that there is a general rule that high resource use is good whilst low resource use is bad. What it means is that we should look at the whole range of human actions and lifestyles from a fresh perspective. We should see the fact that the human species is that part of life which has become technological as a joyous event in the big scheme things. The human species is the expression of life on Earth and its intense desire to survive. The human species should take a step back and look at its achievements in the big scheme of things and be proud of the achievements it has made so far.

The view of the human species as the oppressor of non-human life on Earth, as the destructor of life on Earth, could usefully be transcended. In its place a view of the human species as an expression of life on Earth, as the resource-modifier which can save life on Earth, could be helpfully located.

As with the rest of the universe, the human species is in a continuous state of evolution. In the early stages of its existence the human species was not the magnificent resource-user that it is today. Whilst, in the future the resource use of humans will surely be very different. Large parts of the endowment of resources which we were gifted from previous life-forms to enable us to develop our technology will be used up. For future energy resources we will largely be dependent on technological renewable energy sources. Perhaps in this era of plentiful renewable energy (due to human technology), and a sustainable planet (due to human technology) the idea of the human species as an 'unsustainable' part of life will have been consigned to the dustbin of history. However, that future era depends for its existence on the current actions of the human species in using the resources and developing the technologies which enable this sustainable future. In other words, this future depends on the current perceptions of the human species as the unsustainable destructor of the Earth's resources.

Does being 'green' entail a particular attitude to life on Earth? This is a complex question. After all, we have already seen that it could be the case that all of the actions that lead to the development of technology (and thereby sustainability) are 'green'. And these actions would typically be underpinned by attitudes which are themselves not what one would probably want to call 'green'.

I suggest that we need to distinguish two different spheres of 'greenness'. Firstly, there are the actions which are 'green' when viewed from the perspective of the human species as a whole. Secondly, there are the actions which are 'green' when viewed from the perspective of an individual human. We have largely been concerned with 'green' actions at the level of the human species, and we have seen that these actions can contain a disparate range of attitudes.

When it comes to an individual human it seems that it is appropriate to refer to a 'green' attitude as something quite specific. This attitude will probably include an appreciation of the interconnectedness of all life on Earth, respect for non-human life-forms, and a desire to tread fairly lightly on the Earth (that is – to live 'sustainably' within the human realm).

In the absence of such a 'green' attitude it would be hard to imagine that someone would really be 'green'. Using very few resources is not itself an indicator of 'greenness' – one could use very few resources because of a lack of money or because one is imprisoned. Similarly, one could use few resources but spend one's days torturing animals, as already noted. When the focus is on an individual human, being 'green' seems to require a 'green' attitude. It is likely that ever since the first humans evolved that there have been 'green' humans.

There is clearly a possible conflict between the attitudes of an individual human who is 'green' and the attitudes which are 'green' at the level of the human species. Many attitudes which are 'green' at the level of the human species will not be the same attitudes as those that characterise an individual 'green' human.

Let us return to the issue of sustainability within human society – the 'narrow' notion of sustainability. In this realm sustainability is just about minimising (even 'eradicating') human impacts. There is an even narrower use of the notion of 'sustainability' within human society which refers simply to *the attempt to maintain living standards.* So, there is talk of fossil fuels being 'unsustainable' because they will run out and human living standards are currently dependent on their use. In this use of the term, sustainability is simply the continuous availability of resources to maintain human living standards. If something is 'unsustainable' it means that a replacement source needs to be found so that living standards can be maintained.

So, if water use in an area is unsustainable it will need to be sourced from elsewhere, or a desalinisation plant will need to be built. If cod supplies are unsustainable then an alternative species should be caught to maintain the supply of fish for human consumption.

The most important notion of sustainability is surely not this 'very narrow' notion of sustaining living standards within human society. It is also surely not the 'narrow' notion of minimising human impacts – this notion is focused on the human species and disregards the evolutionary progression of life on Earth which gave rise to the human species, and it also disregards the evolutionary interplay between the Earth and the Sun. The most important notion of sustainability is the wider notion which we have been exploring – sustaining the living conditions of the biosphere to keep them habitable for life.

So, to be 'green' is not to be focused solely on the human realm – human impacts and/or the sustainability of human resource use. To be 'green' is to have a particular attitude to life on Earth (at the level of an individual human), to be focused on all of this life, and to be concerned with the sustainability of the conditions of the Earth's biosphere (at the 'broader' level). The sustainability of life on Earth is compatible with a period of 'unsustainability' in the human realm. More than this, the sustainability of life on Earth seems to be *dependent on* such a period of 'unsustainability'. For, without such 'green' actions the development of technology, the technology which can save life on Earth by maintaining the state of the biosphere, would not be developed.

I have focused on one particular aspect of the value of technology to life on Earth – maintaining the temperature of the atmosphere as the non-technological homeostatic regulatory capacity of life on Earth weakens. However, technology has much more value than this. Even after the human species starts to regulate the temperature of the Earth's atmosphere, and thereby brings sustainability to the Earth, there will still be immense dangers to the continuation of life on Earth which can only be overcome by technology. For example, it is inevitable that there is a massive asteroid which is on course to collide with the Earth sometime in the future. Such a collision would be an immense danger to the survival of complex-life on Earth. However, such a dangerous outcome could be averted if the technology is developed which can 'throw' the asteroid onto a different course.

Even when life on Earth has won the battle with the Sun via human technological regulation of the atmosphere, and also technologically defended itself against asteroid strikes, there is still a need for yet more technology. For, in an evolving universe, ultimately the Sun will eventually expire and life on

Earth will be in grave peril. In the distant future only technology can save life on Earth from extinction. The human species can be the ultimate saviour of life on Earth by designing spacecraft which can transport humans and non-human planetary life-forms to other solar systems.

Being 'green' and valuing the future survival of life on Earth means embracing the wonder that is human technology.

'Green' Spirituality

To be 'green' is to have as one's focus not the well-being of the human species alone, but to have as one's focus the well-being of all life on Earth. I have suggested that 'green actions' at the level of the human species involve a range of different attitudes and actions. You might not be convinced that the human species as a whole is acting in a 'green' manner when it is acting in a way which is unsustainable in the narrow sense. That is to say, you might not be convinced that the human species is acting in a 'green' way when human lifestyles have significant impacts on the biosphere and are dependent on resources which will run out.

I have tried to shake you out of this way of thinking and to get you to focus on the 'broad' notion of sustainability within which the sustainability of the biosphere of the Earth is of paramount importance. I have suggested that when this is our focus sustainability requires short-term human actions which are 'unsustainable' in the 'narrow' use of the term. If being 'green' is *acting in a way which is in the interests of all of the life-forms which exist on the Earth* then these 'unsustainable' (in the 'narrow' sense) actions are 'green'/sustainable actions.

However, I have also claimed that there is another use of the term 'being green' which is centred on a particular way of being in the world. An individual can be thought of as 'being green' if they have a particular attitude to all of the life on Earth; maybe even a particular attitude to the entire universe. This attitude is perhaps aptly described as being under the realm of 'green spirituality'.

There is a curious aspect to 'green spirituality'. For, whilst this attitude concerns the totality of life on Earth, and perhaps the entire universe, the attitude itself resides in a single person. This attitude directs the way this person lives their life. A person grounded in 'green spirituality' is likely to have reverence for all life, to be attuned to the seasons, to tread lightly on the Earth, and to have respect for their fellow life-forms.

At first glance such an attitude seems to be a great thing – to be in the interests of the life-forms of the Earth. Surely, one would think, if all humans had the attitude of 'green spirituality' this would be great news for all of the non-human life-forms on the Earth, and would probably be good news for humans too.

However, our explorations of the broader notion of sustainability have made it clear that the future survival of life on Earth is dependent on the development and deployment of human technology. Would such technology be developed by humans if all humans had the attitude of 'green spirituality'? I doubt that this would be the case as the central tenets of 'green spirituality' are seemingly opposed to human technological interventions into the 'natural' order of things, and opposed to the extensive resource use and 'exploitation' of planetary resources which enabled the development of technology.

If this is right, then the pervasiveness of 'green spirituality' would not be in the interests of life on Earth. So, in a sense, it is actually in the interests of life on Earth to be 'exploited' by the human species. So, I am suggesting that whilst the individual attitude of 'green spirituality' is focused on the good of all of life/the good of the universe, if such an attitude pervaded humanity it would be very harmful for life on Earth/life in the universe; this clearly wouldn't be a good thing.

What does all of this mean? I am not suggesting that 'green spirituality' is an undesirable thing. Rather, I am suggesting that from an evolutionary perspective, and when our focus is the good of the totality of life on Earth, that other attitudes are required. Attitudes which at first glance appear to be antithetical to the interests of life on Earth actually turn out to be in the interests of life on Earth.

The attitude of 'green spirituality' is firmly centred on the role of the human species in an evolving universe, and the importance and value of life on Earth. Indeed, this attitude greatly values the continued existence of life on Earth. The only question is whether *other attitudes* are actually required to fulfil this objective. I have suggested that the seeming opposition between 'green spirituality' and 'technology/intense resource use' means that the future survival of life on Earth is dependent on attitudes other than 'green spirituality'. Herein resides the 'curiousness' of the attitude of 'green spirituality'.

It is perhaps to be hoped that in the future a new attitude arises which combines the best aspects of 'green spirituality' with the reality that the development of human technology is of paramount importance for the continued existence of life on Earth. Perhaps this attitude could be called 'green-tech spirituality'.

In the remaining pages I have provided some 'food for thought' for you. Perhaps, these simple words could be some of the tenets of 'green-tech spirituality'.

To be 'green' is to be at harmony with the universe

To be 'green' is to let the universe flow through you without resistance

To be 'green' is to have respect for all life-forms

To be 'green' is to see the wonder of the Earth

To be 'green' is to see yourself in all that lives

To be 'green' is to be at peace

To be 'green' is to see the purpose in
everything that exists

To be 'green' is to sway with the wind and flow with the stream

To be 'green' is to be grateful for the bounty of the Earth

To be 'green' is to be focused on the future survival
of life on Earth

To be 'green' is to appreciate the positive role that the human species plays on the Earth

To be 'green' is to appreciate that the human species and its activities are wholly part of life on Earth

To be 'green' is to see the bigger picture

To be 'green' can be a particular personal attitude,
but it can also be to appreciate that...

...in the bigger scheme of things to be 'green' can be to have one of a range of different attitudes and actions

To be 'green' is to appreciate the evolving nature of the solar system – the Earth, life on Earth, the Sun...

To be 'green' is to be in awe of the technology that can bring sustainability to the planet and save life from extinction

To be 'green' is to be a fan of renewable energy
(and other technologies too)

To be 'green' is to appreciate the common striving
of all life on Earth to survive

To be 'green' is to fully appreciate and value the
wonder that is life on Earth

To be 'green' is to appreciate the value of the past,
the present and the future

To be 'green' is to seek to protect the future
survival of life on Earth

To be 'green' is to appreciate the value of the industrial revolution and the value of resource use by humans

To be 'green' is to appreciate the value of everything that exists

To be 'green' is to appreciate the wonder of the universe, the universe that brought the human species into existence, and to appreciate that the universe is fulfilling its objectives through the actions of the human species

To be 'green'...........

Other books by the author:

Is the Human Species Special? : Why human-induced global warming could be in the interests of life

Should I be a Vegetarian? : A personal reflection on meat-eating, vegetarianism and veganism

How Much of Man is Natural? : Two versions of the international prize-winning essay

The Purpose of the Environmental Crisis :
A Reinterpretation of Hölderlin's Philosophy

What is the Problem of Consciousness? :
Materialism, Awareness & What-it-is-likeness

www.ingramcontent.com/pod-product-compliance
Lightning Source LLC
Chambersburg PA
CBHW071418040426
42445CB00012BA/1204